The Eight Brothers

Author: Awakened Prince
Illustrator: Awakened Prince

Published by
Wholesome Vision ©
March, 2017

The Eight Brothers
Publisher: Wholesome Vision ©
Author: Awakened Prince
Illustrator: Awakened Prince

1405 Bodega Way #5 Diamond Bar
CA 91765, USA
Tel: 1-909-638-7179
Fax: 1-626-839-5333
Website of Wholesome Vision:
WholesomeVision.com

ISBN: 978-1-945892-00-4
First U.S. Edition

Eight brothers live under one roof:
one is sharp, one is dim,
five do business out front,
and the last one
keeps tabs on everything.

Who are they?

"Eight brothers under one roof"
all add up to one person.

Sounds strange, right?

"Under one roof" means
they all live in one house.

Can you guess what the "house" is?

That's right, it's your body!

The "brothers" (we could also say sisters!) stand for the different parts of what we call our "Great Mind."

Your mind is much more than you realize and that's why we call it the Great Mind.

Every one of us relies on eight forms of consciousness to live a normal life.

So the Great Mind can be divided into eight parts, the eight brothers.

The eight forms of consciousness work in unison all the time, like an experienced dance team, who each have their own job to do.

Brothers One to Five
"doing business out front"
are the eye-consciousness,

The Eight Brothers

the ear-consciousness,

the nose-consciousness,

the tongue-consciousness,

and the body-consciousness.

These are our senses—sight, hearing, smell, taste, and touch—and they interact with the outside world like busy bees, constantly giving us information about the world around us when we're awake.

The one who understands and analyses all the information supplied by these five brothers is Brother Six, the mental-consciousness.

He keeps a close watch, weighing and considering everything the first five brothers do, like a sharp manager.

He's what we think of as our mind.

Day to day, the mental-consciousness
tells us he is our real, ultimate Self.

But if he were really in control, why
would he let himself experience the
suffering of birth, sickness, aging,
and death again and again as we go
through lifetimes one after the other?

Shouldn't he be able to put a stop to
all this and free himself from all the
difficulty and discomfort?

But he can't.

The mental-consciousness is fickle;
his likes and dislikes can flip in
an instant.

He gets bored easily and likes to
stay entertained.

The mental-consciousness ceases during
dreamless sleep, so obviously it is not
something eternal.

Some people teach that the mental-
consciousness will go on to future lives.

They mistake it for the real Self. They
want to believe that this "self-knowing
self" will last forever, but it doesn't.

The final two of the eight brothers
manage things behind the scenes
and we are totally unaware of them.

One of them, Brother Seven, is
called "manas" or the "seventh
consciousness."

He is very quick and responsive.

Like a top-notch butler, he takes
care of everything in the house and
makes decisions whenever necessary
while staying invisible.

The other unseen brother, Brother
Eight, is called the Buddha-Essence.

His formal name is "tathāgatagarbha."
(See if you can say that out loud!)

Sometimes he's also called the
"eighth-consciousness" or the
"foundational-consciousness."

Brother Eight seems dim and
unresponsive but is extremely
important.

We'll talk more about him later.

The Eight Brothers

Day to day, it is actually manas –
Brother Seven – who decides when
to close up shop and tells Brothers
One to Six to close all the doors
and stop receiving guests so we
can fall asleep.

However, neither Brother Seven
nor Brother Eight rests after we
fall asleep.

In fact, they never take even a
moment's break—EVER.

Since he is awake all the time, manas is the one who makes the final decision about everything we do.

For example, when a person is sound asleep, if manas senses any noticeable change in the environment, he wakes up Brother Six—the mental-consciousness—right away to find out what is going on.

He also believes that he is the real "Self."

The Eight Brothers

However, among the eight brothers, only Brother Eight, the Buddha-Essence (the tathāgatagarbha), lives forever and is unaffected by old age, death, or any kind of suffering.

Like the air we breathe, the Buddha-Essence is formless and invisible yet it is the central core of our existence.

While manas isn't the real Self of a being, he does one very important thing.

When a person's body is no longer usable, manas will decide to move to another one.

Since manas believes the Buddha-Essence is part of himself, he drags it with him through many lifetimes in different bodies.

When the manas drags the Buddha-Essence along with it through endless rounds of rebirth, the first five brothers— the consciousnesses of the senses—are unable to follow them.

As we all know, a dead person has no feelings and perceptions, which means that our mental-consciousness, the sixth brother, also ceases at death and does not go on to the next life.

The Eight Brothers

While we are alive, the Buddha-Essence keeps records of everything we do in each life, in the way a black box in an aircraft stores all the transmitted data.

Applying the law of cause and effect – also called karma – to our conduct, the Buddha-Essence enables the creation of a new body of an animal, a human, a celestial being, or whatever form we deserve based on what we have done in our previous lives.

Obviously, the "records" that the Buddha- Essence of each person contains are unique to that person, since no two beings have ever done exactly the same things or had the same experiences.

Think of how even identical twins are not totally alike in their personalities, hobbies, capabilities and appearances.

This is also why some people display particular gifts, sometimes at very young ages.

The famous Chinese poet Li Bai was writing great poems at the age of ten.

The great European composer Beethoven held concerts in Köln, Germany at the age of eight.

They displayed such brilliance because the seeds of their gifts had been stored in their own Buddha-Essence and brought forward from their previous lives.

These are examples where very good things came from previous lives.

Not only is every sentient being—people, animals, birds, insects, etc.—created by its own Buddha-Essence, but everything in the physical world—galaxies, planets, mountains, and rivers—is created collectively by the Buddha-Essences of karmically-related sentient beings working together.

The Buddha-Essence is indeed the most amazing yet invisible magician.

It is our real Self.

The Buddha-Essence itself isn't changed by the karmic records.

Like a cup that can hold different drinks, it's the one thing that stays the same, regardless of its contents, life after life.

A Buddha is someone who knows all knowledge stored in his Buddha-Essence, has perfected the merits and virtues, and possesses the ability to utilize all the features the Buddha-Essence has to offer.

But the Buddha-Essence is formless and shapeless, so how can we find it?

Think of how our eyes cannot see germs because they are very small, or distant galaxies because they are too far.

We need the help of microscopes and telescopes. Similarly, to "see" the Buddha-Essence, we need to have a special tool, the "eye of wisdom."

So how can we open and use our wisdom-eye?

In everyday life, we should treat people with kindness and respect, cultivate tolerance and compassion within ourselves, respect the Three Jewels, and accept the Buddha's teachings with faith.

If you can do all these consistently, your wisdom-eye will soon awaken.

By cultivating the Buddha Dharma with diligence, your wisdom-eye will open when all the conditions are right, and you will be able to "see" the Buddha-Essence, the invisible magician in you.

You may wonder:

Why do we need to see the
"invisible magician"?

Isn't it enough just to be a
good kid?

Being a good kid is of course the
right thing to do.

But even a good kid has all kinds of
records from past lives stored in the
Buddha-Essence, which will result
in endless rounds of birth, life, and
death – your karma.

Imagine yourself stuck on an
uncontrollable Ferris wheel that
cannot be stopped, one that
brings you through many kinds of
environments.

It may be easy to be a virtuous person
for one life, but is it possible to stick
to the right course over trillions of
lifetimes in different situations?

All it takes is one bad friend or one
slip, and you'll have to live with
the painful consequences of your
misconduct for a very, very long time.

In that case, would it still be easy to
be a good kid?

What keeps this Ferris wheel of rebirth
going are the mental consciousness and
the manas when they wrongly think
they are the real and eternal Self.

They think being a good person can halt
the powerful karmic force that drives the
Ferris wheel.

Instead, we must seek the Buddha-Essence
because it is the only mind entity that is
everlasting and unchanging over time.

By learning the correct Buddha Dharma,
we can change the karmic forces stored
in the Buddha-Essence by correcting and
purifying manas from the effects of any
bad things we've done.

As we change the good and bad
karmic forces with pure practices and
enlightening insights, the Ferris wheel
will begin to function properly and come
under our control.

When it does, we can move toward
becoming a Buddha.

Potentially, every one of us can become a Buddha.

To be more precise, any sentient being can become a Buddha. So we are all equal in terms of our chance of attaining Buddhahood.

When we become a Buddha— like Buddha Shakyamuni, Buddha Amitabha, or any other Buddhas—we will acquire all knowing wisdom.

As a Buddha, we will each have the power to choose our rebirth in any world and become any kind of sentient being, so that we can teach people anywhere about the wisdom of liberation from the uncontrolled cycle of rebirth.

A Buddha is omniscient, as he knows everything about the universe and the planet we live on, as well as everything we have done over the countless lives we have lived.

As we know, everything we do is recorded in the Buddha-Essence and a Buddha has the wisdom to access the information stored in it, like you can find the information on your computer.

To become a Buddha you have to perfect your merits and wisdom, as well as assist countless other sentient beings on their way toward Buddhahood.

If you can cultivate the Buddha Dharma and learn all about the Eight Consciousnesses in each and every life you live, then you can gradually replace negative habit energy, such as craving, egoism, arrogance, and aversion, with the seeds of pure actions.

As long as you continue to
cultivate the Buddha Dharma
and follow the noble path of
bodhisattvas, you will eventually
attain Buddhahood.

When you become a Buddha,
you will be able to benefit
countless other people and help
liberate them from the suffering
that comes with birth, aging,
sickness, and death.

You can also bring them never-
ending wisdom that leads to
true liberation and ultimate
happiness.

Would you want to be able to
do that one day?

If you really want to become
a Buddha, you can make the
following vow every day:

*May I acquire the unsurpassed
merits and wisdom of a Buddha,
so that I can help liberate all
sentient beings from endless rounds
of rebirth. To achieve this, I sincerely
vow to cultivate the Buddha
Dharma and learn all there is to
know about the Buddha-Essence.*

八個兄弟
共一胎
———

The Eight Brothers

八個兄弟一個胎

一個伶俐一個呆

八個兄弟共一胎

五個門前作買賣
一個家裡把帳開

我們每個人都有八個心識，猶如親兄弟形影不離，合作無間。有兩位看似在幕後而不為人知的兄弟：伶俐的「末那識」像個幕後大總管，看顧一家子大大小小事情，隨時裁量決定。看似呆呆的「如來藏」，我們最後再詳細說祂。

在幕前風光得意的「眼識、耳識、鼻識、舌識、身識」五個小兄弟，每天在門口接觸外界的人事地物，忙碌得像是做生意的夥計一樣。陪伴在夥計身旁，緊盯著每件買賣作帳，斤斤計較個停的，就是八面玲瓏的「意識」大掌櫃。

八個兄弟共一胎

晚上末那識決定打烊了，叫意識大掌櫃和五識等夥計們都不用再忙了，對於外界不要再了別。然而，末那識和如來藏卻不休息，一旦發生任何大狀況，末那識就趕緊叫起意識等六兄弟查明狀況。

末那識做主決定一切的事，
從來不知道如來藏的存在，
誤以為自己是「我」。意識
心總認為自己是我，然而意
識「我」領受著生老病死的
痛苦，如果這「我」是真實
的，為何要讓自己受苦呢？
是否至少能夠不老死變異，
也不受痛苦？八兄弟中，唯
有如來藏一直存在，不會
老，也不會死，也不會苦。

八個兄弟共一胎

如來藏祂就像我們呼吸的空氣一樣，看不見形狀，卻與我們十分密。祂從不躲藏，一直與兄弟們長相左右。每一有情都由各自的如來藏所出生，銀河星系、山河大地也是由大家的如來藏共同感應而變生。祂是位神奇的「無形魔術師」。

末那識總是沈醉於存在感，當色身不能用時，末那識就繼續換到下一世。末那識誤以為如來藏是自己的一部分，帶著如來藏去輪迴。如來藏把我們每一世做過的善惡事統統收存起來，猶如飛航資料記錄器「黑」盒子，再依照這些記錄，讓我們來世變成貓、狗、人、天人等等，這就是宇宙中的因果業報輪迴的公平法則。

末那識帶著如來藏去繼續輪
迴時，前六識無法跟去。人
死後，任何覺受都不存在，
意識無法去到下一世。

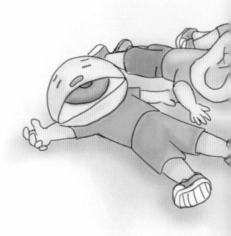

八個兄弟共一胎

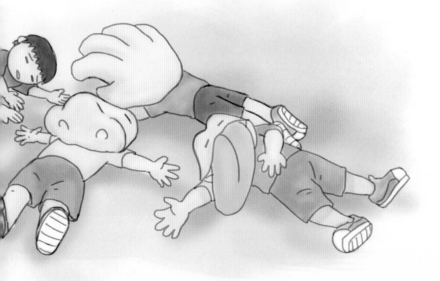

意識從小到大一直改變，喜歡與討厭的對象可能一夕之間就全數改變。當睡覺無夢時，意識就消失了。這意識不會永恆不變。堅持意識可以去到未來世的人，是由於貪愛意識的覺知性，錯認祂是真實「我」。佛法說，不論未來生的意識可否知道前一生的意識，這意識還是變異無常，永遠不是真實「我」。

每一個人的如來藏「黑盒子」裡的記錄也各自不同。即便是長得非常相像的雙胞胎，個性、愛好、能力、長相也都不同。

中國詩人李白十歲精通詩書，德國音樂家貝多芬八歲在科隆舉行演奏會，他們的才能種子都是從過去世帶來的，老早就存在如來藏裏。

如來藏無形無相，誰能看見祂呢？我們的肉眼看不見微小的細菌與遙遠的星河，要藉由顯微鏡與望遠鏡，才能看到這些事物。神奇的如來藏也要藉由佛法的智慧，才能看得見。

想知道如何睜開智慧眼嗎？
日常生活好好待人接物，培
養寬容心，慈悲心，尊敬三
寶，相信佛陀，開啟智慧的
機緣就到了。精進學習正確
的佛法，假以時日，因緣條
件成熟，就能睜開慧眼，
看見自己的如來藏「無形魔
術師」！

是否有疑問：

為何要看到「無形魔術師」？

只要努力做個好孩子，不就好了嗎？

八個兄弟共一胎

表面上是如此。但隨著如來藏黑盒子的業力牽引，生了死、死了生，像個無法掌控的摩天輪，永無止盡的持續輪轉，感覺上很沒意思。一輩子當好人可能很容易，那一萬億兆輩子呢？只要一次遇到惡友而失足，未來就是受苦，如何再當好孩子呢？這輪迴摩天輪的樞紐在於末那識與意識都錯認了真實「我」，作好事與作好人並不能停止失控的業力摩天輪，唯有如來藏才具備我們所追求的永恆真實的體性。學習真實佛法，讓末那識更加清淨，如來藏黑盒子才會轉變，將善惡業力成為清淨願力，讓摩天輪配合著清淨願力而正常運轉。

我們每個人將來都可以成佛，大地的任何一位眾生都可以成佛，大家在成佛上都是平等的。可以像釋迦牟尼佛、阿彌陀佛，任何一尊佛，智慧無邊，依照自己的願力，能夠扮演世界上任何有情的角色，幫助那裏的眾生，讓大家得到真實的解脫智慧。

佛對宇宙的形成、對我們
生活的地球、銀河系的來
龍去脈，無所不知。佛知
道我們上一世、上上世、
再上上世、更無量的上上
世的一切，因為這些都記
錄在如來藏「黑盒子」
裏，而佛有解讀任何一個
「黑盒子」的智慧。

當然，「成佛」必須具足圓滿的福德和智慧，幫助如同數不盡的恆河沙子般這麼多的有情眾生一起邁向成佛之道。生生世世學佛，熏聞八識正理，將原本如來藏儲存的貪心計較、心量狹小、驕傲自慢、憎恨眾生的種種雜染習氣種子，汰換成清淨的種子，持續進步，就會一直走在佛法的智慧大道上，最後一定會成佛。

成佛能夠幫助許許多多的
人離開生老病死的痛苦，
讓大家都能得到真正的解
脫幸福與泉湧的智慧，你
覺得歡喜嗎？

記得每天都發願：
我要像佛一樣，
福慧兩足尊，
以後也要成佛，
來幫助一切的眾生！
我要學佛，
找到如來藏喲！